Bird  for Beginners

A Beginner's Guide to the Basics of Birding so That You Can Pick the Right Tools and Go Out and Find and Identify Remarkable Birds or Attract Them to Your Own Yard

By Eli Leander

circumstances is the author responsible for any losses, direct or indirect, which are incurred as a result of the use of information contained within this document, including, but not limited to, —errors, omissions, or inaccuracies.

Contents

Thank you for buying this book and I hope that you will find it useful. If you will want to share your thoughts on this book, you can do so by leaving a review on the Amazon page, it helps me out a lot.

INTRODUCTION

Picture yourself lying in your bed. The early morning sun is just peeking through your window. Together with the sun, you hear the harmonic tune of birds chirping their "good mornings" to each other-- and to you! Have you ever asked yourself what those birds looked like? Why are they close enough for you to hear? What intriguing qualities they have about them?

Bird watching is a sport that has actually been around for many years. Actually, today, bird watching is the 2nd fastest-growing hobby in America, bested just by gardening. An entire new language has emerged together with it. Some people additionally describe bird watching just as "birding" and individuals who do it as "birders."

Individuals of all ages take pleasure in looking for the birds of their region, watching them in their natural habitat, and taking pleasure in the songs they have to provide. Birds can be remarkable animals with much to provide those who care to study their lives. Much could be learned from where they roost, how they fly, and what they sing. We can even go so far as to state that watching birds can uncover aspects of nature and the elegance that exists in nature.

" I once had a sparrow alight upon my shoulder momentarily, while I was hoeing in a village garden, and I felt that I was more distinguished by that situation that I should have been by any epaulet I might have worn."

~ Henry David Thoreau

Birding could be done anywhere. You can discover all sorts of species in your local park, any forest, and even in your own yard!

Nobody understands the sights and sounds of nature quite like a bird watcher. By taking a half-second look at a little darting collection of black, yellow, and white feathers and incorporating a musical note that sounds something like "chirp," a birder can tell you, not just the general species of that bird, yet she or he can narrow it down to the precise bird.

To distinguish amongst the 900+ species of birds discovered in the U.S., birders need to rapidly process a lot of information on color patterns, call notes, and even the shapes of bills. They need to understand what to key in on when they see an odd bird, noting its general shape, how it moves through a bush or tree, and the shape of its wings. Such sensory work-outs aid to develop excellent visual and hearing acuity amongst birders. In fact, birders are usually a lot more watchful than the typical individual.

To the starting bird watcher, this may look like an amazing task that they may never ever have the ability to accomplish. Attempting to recognize even typical species can be exceptionally discouraging, and lots of people quit before they ever really start.

Discovering birds and recognizing them can take place in an instant. A little black bird flashes up to the top of a bush. You get your binoculars and begin reading your guidebook. You take another look at the bird, flip back a page or more ... all of a sudden, the bird is gone, yet there is a different one lower in the bush. All that page riffling and binocular lifting starts once again.

Birding can make you more acquainted with the natural beauty of the world and maybe will lead you to appreciate how rapidly that elegance is being lost. Birding can coax you into the brand-new country and allows you to take in all the fresh air and outstanding scenery that you can hold. Crucial, however, is the truth that birding is just too much fun to be missed out on.

The kind of information provided here is second nature to a skilled birder, yet it can take numerous months of hard work for the starting bird watcher to comprehend these ideas and methods. Even with the information spelled out here, you still need to supply a good bit of patience and sweat to turn into one of the really tuned-in nature watchers.

We have actually attempted to strip away a bit of the mystique of Bird watching and expose the bare fundamentals; however, practice and patience are just as crucial to bird watching as they are to sports, music, and other leisure activities. You can't expect to record 150 various species on your initial outing (though this will be possible in the future) or to recognize all those confusing birds. You'll need to work at it.

This book is meant to help you get beyond the aggravating early stage. It's a crash course in the fundamentals of bird watching or "birding." Ideally, with the assistance of this book, you'll be well on your way to higher enjoyment of the world around you because birding concentrates on a few of the most incredible animals in the world.

Birds are extremely visual creatures - much like people - and some species wear spectacular combinations of yellows, blues, reds, blacks, and greens, making them more apparent to the naked eye. They additionally can be found in a wide array of shapes and forms, which adds substantially to the pleasures of Bird watching.

You simply may discover that bird watching isn't just enjoyable, it's a learning experience too! Birding gets you outdoors, provides you with exercise, makes you think, and sharpens your observational abilities. Keep reading and take notes as we take a look at bird watching for beginners!

Chapter 1: Why Watch Birds?

Birds have long thrilled folks all over the world because of their elegance and their power of flight. Birds are everywhere, and everywhere they are different. Birds are mystical, wonderful, and often incredibly elusive.

Historically, they used to be considered omens. The ancient Romans thought that the flights and calls of birds might predict the future. Today, contemporary science still utilizes birds as a type of oracle. Alterations in bird populations can mirror the health of the environment.

Birding additionally fulfills another fundamental instinct-- the mission for knowledge. Birding has to do with obtaining knowledge. Not just about birds' names, yet additionally about their songs, their habits, and how they connect to the rest of nature. It's an ideal opportunity to take pleasure in a unique human pleasure-- the successful exercise of lore.

Actually, amateur birders typically get to make real contributions to scientific knowledge. Today, much of what ornithology understands about birds has actually originated from the observations of regular yet devoted birders.

Some birds are indicator species, like the USA's national bird, the bald eagle. They forecast ecological conditions. The understanding of birds can aid us in planning a greater, more lasting relationship with nature.

Perhaps we watch birds since they are out there: anywhere we go, birds are there, typically active while we are active, sleeping while we sleep. In our own yards, we lure them with bird feeders and birdhouses, and by putting shrubs, water, and proper plants in the landscape. More than any creature other than maybe bugs, birds noticeably share our outdoor area, and if we need to travel miles and sit silently for patient hours in order to see an uncommon or evasive bird, that makes it a treasure hunt.

We enjoy treasure hunts and we enjoy novelty. Birds offer both. While numerous birds have extremely wide ranges, the birds of one country tend to vary from the birds of another; even if you discover the birds at home rather common, you are going to be delighted by unknown birds when you travel. You will see the exact same kind of bird in different areas, however, the birds will be different.

Birds are wonderful. Their dazzling hues provide a companion to their color vision. Birds flash past in every shade from emerald to vermillion, stunning as showy flower blossoms yet generally more surprising. A limitless variety of patterns, shapes, and sizes thrill us. Even the typical crow has a charming sheen and particular beauty. Yes, birds are an amazing part of life-- how could we not watch birds?

Bird watching is enjoyable! It offers you an excellent reason to leave your tv behind and venture out into the elements. Want a great reason to go out and go for a walk? Bring along your binoculars. It provides a healthy activity that practically anybody can take pleasure in. You do not require great knees like you would need for snowboarding. You do not even need to be able to venture beyond your own garden.

Birding is additionally the perfect solitary sport. There's a special enjoyment in heading out alone to bird. Your mind calms down. Your senses open, and all nature appears to become your buddy. Birding is a sport of numerous moods, and it serves the causes of friendship and solitude similarly well.

Be advised, nevertheless, birding can be addictive. You might find yourself obsessed with some uncommon species that might have been reported in your area. You find yourself getting up earlier and earlier to put in a couple of hours of birding before work. You start taking a look at your landscaping in an entirely new way as you begin planting more bird-friendly plants, setting up feeders and birdbaths and minimizing the use of damaging chemicals.

As we have actually claimed, birds can be remarkable animals. If you've never ever watched them previously, simply try for a couple of minutes in the morning light. Take a look at how they soar through the air. Listen to their early morning songs. You can discover excellent peace and excellent enlightenment in birds. How would you be able to really delight in these animals unless you watched them? It's time to get going with bird watching!

Chapter 2: What Equipment Do You Require?

The very best part about bird watching is that you do not require much in the way of tools to do it successfully. You ought to simply begin with an excellent set of binoculars, a guidebook, a note pad, and a camera. Let's take a look at each part separately.

Binoculars

You require binoculars to see the birds better. You will quickly find an ironic truth. The very best birders have the very best binoculars-- despite the fact that they can recognize a bird 100 yards away by its shape. Beginners with an inexpensive binocular see a fuzzy ball of feathers, and they do not have an idea which bird it is. There is an incredible distinction between a $59 binocular and a $900 binocular.

Binoculars are a birder's eyes on the world, and they can considerably impact the quality of a bird outing. Great binoculars produce excellent birding, while bad binoculars can result in missed birds and extreme headaches caused by blurred images, double vision, and eye strain.

Binoculars can be found in various shapes and forms and carry such descriptions as "roof prism," "close focus," "armor coated," and so on. At the outset, you do not need to spend a lot of time analyzing this arcane lexicon. If you truly get hooked on bird-watching, you can find out more about binoculars later on and trade in for a much better pair. A good pair of binoculars will run you around $60 depending upon where you live. There are a couple of easy guidelines to think about and questions to ask when buying your initial set of binoculars.

1. Make certain the power (or magnification) is at least 7-power. The power is the first number given in the numerical notation that explains binoculars. For instance, a "7 X 35" set of "glasses" will make things look like if they are 7 times as close as they really are. Seven-power binoculars are about the minimum required to see birds well. Binoculars 10-power or more powerful can be tough for some birders to hold steady.

2. Make certain that the 2nd number ("35" for a "7 X 35" set of glasses) is at least 5 times as big as the power (e.g., "7 X 35," "8 X 40," and so on). This 2nd number illustrates the size, in millimeters, of the big lens that faces the object of interest - the "objective" lens. The bigger this lens is, the highcr the amount of light the binoculars collect, and hence, the simpler it will be to see qualities in dim light or on a dull-colored bird.

3. Are the binoculars too heavy for you to carry and utilize for at least 2 hours straight? Do not wind up with a hunchback since your binoculars act like a yoke.

4. Can you bend the barrels of the binoculars relatively easily? To check to see if they are too flexible, spread out the barrels out as far as possible, and after that, keep only one of the barrels. Does the free barrel slip or fall from the spread position? It should not.

5. When held a foot away, do the big objective lenses reflect a bluish or purple tint? If they do, the lenses are color-coated. This coating lowers internal glare in the binoculars and increases the quantity of light that, in fact, comes to your eyes. Inspect the lenses to make certain the coatings are devoid of any blotches or scrapes.

6. Can you bring the barrels of the binoculars close enough together to ensure that the image you see merges into a single, clear image within a single, excellent circle? If the image isn't singular or clear, the binoculars might be out of positioning or the eyepieces might not come close enough together to suit your eyes. These 2 issues might result in eye strain and extreme headaches.

7. Do you wear prescription glasses? If you do, your binoculars ought to have rubber eye cups that fold back. This enables you to place your eyeglasses up closer to the eyepieces of your binoculars and offers you a much bigger field of vision.

8. Do the binoculars produce a clear image of things just 20 feet away? Some binoculars do not concentrate on things this close, so you might miss out on the sparrow or warbler that skulks in a neighboring bush.

9. Take a look at an indication with big lettering. Do the letters near to the edge of the field of vision look like accurate and well-formed as the letters in the center of the field of vision? Image distortion towards the edge of binoculars is common in bad binoculars - like looking through a fish-eye lens. Search for a set that has very little distortion

10. When you concentrate on a license plate or little sign 2 blocks away, are the letters and numbers apparent? If they're not, select a different set!

A basic list of what to think about when purchasing binoculars:

- Don't buy compact or pocket-sized binoculars (usually 8 x 21, or 10 x 21) as your main pair for birding. The size and weight are appealing, however no matter how great the optics, compacts offer a lower quality image than mid- or full-size binoculars. Another downside is that many compacts have a narrow field of vision, which makes it really challenging to find and follow birds.

- Don't buy zoom binoculars. Expert birders report them as being inferior.

- Do not seek advice on purchasing optics from non-birders. Hikers, hunters, and boaters don't have the same requirements as birders. Taking a look at birds is not the same as taking a look at other wildlife. Pocket binoculars are great for looking throughout a savannah at an elephant or a cheetah, yet they are not appropriate for birding. Marine binoculars supply a sharp, brilliant image, yet are too huge and heavy to bring around throughout the day.

- Don't buy binoculars up until you have actually tried them. Make certain they feel comfy in your hands. Look through them and make certain you get a clear, unblocked view. Various models match various individuals, and each instrument differs. If ordering by mail or online, make certain that you can exchange them.

One thing about binoculars-- you do not constantly need to have the very best specs for bird watching. Any binoculars are better than none at all. The important thing to bear in mind is that you want to have something to amplify the birds you will be trying to find. If you are serious about bird watching, take heed of the pointers for purchasing binoculars provided above. They will be well worth the money!

Practicing Utilizing Your New Binoculars

Before utilizing your binoculars, it is very important to adjust them, so they make up for the varying strengths of your 2 eyes. Take a lens cap and conceal the right objective lens with it. Then look through the left lens and concentrate on an item 30 feet away, utilizing the primary focusing knob situated between the two barrels of your binoculars.

When you have concentrated on the object, move the lens cap from the right lens to the left lens. Look through the right lens at the identical thing (however, do not touch the primary focusing wheel!) If the image you see is not as clear as it looked through the left lens, calibrate it utilizing the focusing ring connected to the right eyepiece of your binoculars. Make note of where you have actually set the focus on the right eyepiece. Now your binoculars are adapted to your eyes and prepared for action.

Next, spend time establishing the hand-eye coordination you'll require to identify birds rapidly. A lot of bird watching is absolutely not like watching football. With bird watching, there's a lot more action - everything is taking place at 1/100 the scale and moves 100 times as rapidly over an endless expanse of space. It requires time for beginning birders to learn the ropes of finding birds with their binoculars. The trick is to find out how to identify a bird with the naked eye, and after that, lift the binoculars up to your eyes without ever taking your eyes off the bird.

Discover a comfy spot at a neighborhood park and hang around simply practicing finding things with your binoculars. At first, set the focus lever on the binoculars so that an item roughly 30 feet away remains in clear view. This is a great average distance from which you can learn to focus the binoculars in and out.

Then begin to search for birds with your naked eyes, and after that, discover them with your binoculars. Just follow the bird around for a while, lowering and raising your binoculars occasionally. Do not stress over recognizing birds yet. Simply watch what they are doing. Shortly, you'll have the ability to find and focus like a pro.

Field Guides

What is a field guide? A field guide is a small book that's loaded with information about birds. It's the next best thing to an expert birder at hand. It illustrates and shows images of the birds, and it tells you which details of each bird to try to find.

A field guide can tell you what types of birds might be in your specific location and offer some exceptional suggestions on what to try to find in your bird watching. If you do not have a field guide, you will not have an idea about what types of birds you will be seeing, so this is vital to have. A field guide will usually cost you around $20.

A field guide consists of photos of birds and ideas for recognizing them. The very best book for brand-new birders is the Peterson Field Guide to Eastern Birds or the Peterson Field Guide to Western Birds. When you end up being knowledgeable about the birds in your area, you will most likely want the National Geographic Field Guide to the Birds of North America 3rd edition. For young birders, I suggest

Peterson First Guide: Birds. It describes 188 typical and conspicuous birds and it will not overwhelm you with a lot of choices. You will additionally wish to take a look at the brand-new Stokes Field Guides.

There has actually been a genuine surge in the number of field guides released about birds over the last couple of years. Up until the late 1960s, the guide most commonly utilized was Roger Tory Peterson's The Birds of Eastern North America, the very first field guide of its kind created. This book actually made bird watching a popular activity by making precise identifications of birds possible.

Today, nevertheless, there are specific field guides offered for certain regions of the nation (Texas even has its own field guide) along with for particular groups of birds, like hawks, gulls, shorebirds, ducks, and others. These specialized books might ultimately make their way into the library of a birding enthusiast. Still, novices need to just think about the comprehensive guides when selecting their first field guide. When buying your initial guide, it is best to start with the one that shows paintings of birds instead of photos. Paintings enable artists to include all differentiating features (called "field marks") that help to recognize a bird in each illustration. Frequently, photos do not show all these marks because of lighting or positioning of the bird. Photographic guides can be an important companion reference, particularly when studying the details of a bird's shape.

When you have actually picked your field guide, do not instantly run off trying to find birds, since what you'll really find instead of birds is trouble and disappointment. Many a field guide has actually spent more time gathering dust than aiding to recognize birds due to the fact that the owner didn't find out how to utilize the guide.

Take a seat with your field guide when you initially get it and read through the full introduction. Next, take a look at a few of the pictures and find out where a few of the common birds you recognize are located in the field guide (i.e., front, back, or middle).

If you wish to end up being a devoted outdoor birder, you'll want a guide that is simple to bring and flip through rapidly. If you are more of a backyard birder, watching local species on your feeders and birdbath, mobility is not as essential.

Field Guide Organization

Various novices tend to detect a bird and instantly open their field guide to the middle pages. They then look to the right 10 pages, look left 10 pages not to discover the bird. Then they look right 20 pages, look left 20 pages, and still without any success. After looking a few more pages left and right, they heave the guide into the air out of disgust and quit on the entire thing.

This occurs due to the fact that the individual hasn't discovered how bird species are arranged in the field guide. It's no surprise they get irritated. Field guides, much like dictionaries and phone books, are purchased according to an accurate system that identifies where various birds lie in the book.

If you were searching for the word "aardvark" in the dictionary, you would not start someplace in the middle, would you? Likewise, if you see a sparrow-like bird resting on the ground, do not start searching through the middle of a field guide due to the fact that all the sparrows lie in the last quarter of field guides.

The majority of guides are approximately arranged in "phylogenetic order." Phylogenetic order is the way scientists categorize all living things (not only birds) based upon their evolutionary history - which animals, according to similarities in their contemporary look, most probably evolved from common ancestors.

You can find out more about this ordering system by reading your field guide. The point is that birds having comparable physical appearances appear really close together in a field guide. You will not discover sparrows on the identical page with hawks or a loon facing a warbler. All sparrows, loons, warblers, hawks, and even gulls and blackbirds lie lots of pages far from one another.

There are 5 vital levels of classification by which all birds are organized. When we describe birds of the identical "species," for instance, a group of 15 blue jays, we are utilizing the most specific level of category.

Similar species are organized into a "genus," then various genera (plural of genus) are organized into a "family," various families are organized into an "order" of birds, and lastly all orders are organized into simply one "class." This is the class "Aves," which in Latin describes all birds. As you might guess, species in the identical genus are more closely related to one another - and look more alike - than species in various genera. Also, families organized in a single order are more comparable to one another than families organized in various orders.

A lot of field guides covering North America consist of about 800-900 species, organized into over 300 genera, organized into 74 various families, organized into simply 20 various orders (guides limited to eastern or western North America have about half as many species). The most sensible classification level for the beginning birder to concentrate on is the family. There are just way too many genera and species out there for a beginner to understand quickly, and identification to a specific order is too broad to be daunting. More significantly, by finding out the standard shape, size, and look of the different families of birds, you will establish the powers of observation that define an excellent birder.

In fact, you most likely understand more about a few of the families than you know. For instance, if you can recognize a laughing gull, you already know a lot about the general shapes and sizes of all the gulls. In a similar way, by understanding what a cardinal looks like, you understand a good bit about buntings, grosbeaks, and other members of this family - specifically that they have extremely thick, pointed bills.

Equipped with the capability to recognize the shapes of the significant bird families and a great local field guide, you can go anywhere in the world and instantly find yourself head and shoulders above non-birders in regards to identification abilities - although you do not have any familiarity or experience with the local birds. So when you initially get your field guide, spend time taking a look at its organization and the manner in which it groups families of birds. Divide your guide into 4 areas utilizing tags or sticky notes. The first quarter is going to consist of the families of big water birds, the 2nd quarter of the big land birds (ending with the woodpeckers), and the last 2 quarters will consist of the little land birds (all in the order "Passeriformes," typically referred to as the "passerines" or "perching birds").

Continue to search for common species that you currently understand and utilize these as a guide for learning the common attributes of other species in the family. Keep in mind, you ought to start birding utilizing your head, not running around chasing evasive thrushes and confusing fall warblers. Look casually, not anxiously, at birds you do not know. Geared up with your spyglasses and dependable field guide, you can now start to get acquainted with all those flitting bundles of feathers.

Notebook

This does not need to be anything elegant. I suggest something smaller than the basic 8 x 11 variety. Bring something that is simple to manage and can be kept on your person without being too invasive.

What do you wish to write down in your notebook? Birds you have actually seen, where you saw them, what they appeared like, what they sounded like, and so on. When you record these observations right when you see (and/or hear) them, you are going to have the ability to better assess your experience in the future.

Camera

While this is not always considered as an important tool for bird watching, I believe it ought to be. If you happen to come across an especially wonderful species of bird and wish to capture it for later study, you might count on your mind, or you might simply snap a photo.

The majority of the world is going digital nowadays. With your digital camera, get one that has the maximum pixels chosen for the very best images. Make certain you have a zoom lens so you can get "up close and personal" with your fine feathered buddies. And, by all means, switch off the flash! Nothing can frighten a bird faster than a flash of light from your camera!

If you have photos of the birds you see, you can additionally do a more extensive analysis of the birds once you get home. With photos, you can dive more deeply into your field guide and record the specific birds you encountered in your exploration.

And just imagine the photo album you can produce! Wonderful!

Anything Else?

The majority of knowledgeable bird watchers highly suggest a hat-- one that covers your head from the sun and makes you less obvious. Any old hat will do. Birding is not a style contest. However, the hat ought to shade your eyes and not interfere with utilizing your binoculars.

A birding vest works, too. You can put your binoculars, your field guide, your pen and note pad, and possibly some insect repellent in the pockets. Hang the vest near the door, and you'll be prepared to get it and have everything you require for bird watching at a moment's notice. One last note, when birding, you ought to wear neutral-colored clothes, not white. The last thing you want is to spook typically skittish animals with vibrantly colored clothes that call attention to the reality that you are there watching them!

Now that you have the appropriate equipment, let's look first at some bird watching rules.

Chapter 3: Emily Post on Bird Watching

Equipped with understanding and enthusiasm, you are now prepared to head into the field and fill your notebook with lots of brand-new species. However, do not let your eagerness get in the way of standard birding rules.

Remember that in order to discover most birds, you will be encroaching on their territory, so tread gently and respect boundaries.

Keep in mind that silence is golden. The eager senses of birds alert them to your presence, typically long before you have an opportunity to see them. Whether alone or in a group, walk as silently as possible and whisper. Take cues from the leader who may signal for quiet as the group comes close to a bird. Peaceful walks will additionally assist when listening for bird calls.

Take additional care when in a potential or active nesting area. It is tough enough for birds to compete with one another for mates and space; human disturbance causes extra tension.

Make certain you are not trespassing on private property. Some bird sanctuaries lie on someone's land, whose owners might not delight in complete strangers with binoculars trekking around their yard. Make certain you have the authorization to bird in advance.

Do not be a peeping Tom! Stay away from pointing your binoculars at other individuals or their houses.

While some birders choose solitude, others bird in groups and take pleasure in sharing their findings. If you are brand-new to birding, do not be shy; there is sure to be a more well-informed birder in the group ready to hand down suggestions and sightings to you.

Most significantly, enjoy yourself! Do not be too worried about finding that rare bird, or identifying more species than last month. Birding is meant to be insightful but also enjoyable.

We feel it is essential here to quote the American Birding Associations "Principles of Birding Ethics":

American Birding Association's PRINCIPLES OF BIRDING ETHICS

Everybody who takes pleasure in birding needs to always appreciate wildlife, its environment, and the rights of others. In any conflict of interest in between birds and birders, the well-being of the birds and their environment comes first.

CODE OF BIRDING ETHICS

1. Promote the well-being of birds and their environment. 1(a) Support the safety of essential bird habitat.

1(b) To stay away from stressing birds or exposing them to risk, exercise restraint and care throughout the observation, photography, sound recording, or recording.

Limit the use of recordings and other approaches of drawing in birds, and never ever utilize such techniques in greatly birded areas, or for drawing in any species that is Endangered, or of Special Concern, or is uncommon in your area;

Keep well back from nests and nesting colonies, roosts, display locations, and crucial feeding sites. In such delicate locations, if there is a requirement for prolonged observation, photography or recording, make an effort to utilize a blind or hide, and make the most of natural cover.

Utilize artificial light moderately for recording or photography, specifically for close-ups.

1(c) Before advertising the existence of a rare bird, assess the possibility for disturbance to the bird, its surroundings, and other individuals in the location, and continue just if access can be managed, disturbance reduced, and approval has been acquired from private land-owners. The sites of uncommon nesting birds ought to be disclosed just to the appropriate conservation authorities.

1(d) Remain on roads, tracks, and courses where they exist; otherwise, keep habitat disturbance to a minimum.

2. Regard the law and the rights of others. 2(a) Do not go into private property without the owner's explicit authorization.

2(b) Follow all laws, guidelines, and regulations governing using roadways and public locations, both at home and abroad.

2(c) Practice common courtesy in contacts with other individuals. Your excellent behavior will produce goodwill with birders and non-birders alike.

3. Make sure that feeders, nest structures, and other artificial bird environments are safe.

3(a) Keep dispensers, water, and food tidy, and devoid of decay or illness. It is essential to feed birds constantly throughout severe weather conditions.

3(b) Maintain and clean nest structures routinely.

3(c) If you are drawing in birds to an area, guarantee the birds are not exposed to predation from cats and other domestic animals, or threats presented by artificial threats.

4. Group birding, whether arranged or unplanned, calls for special care.

Each person in the group, in addition to the responsibilities defined in Items # 1 and # 2, has obligations as a Group Member.

4(a) Regard the interests, rights, and abilities of fellow birders, along with individuals taking part in other legitimate outdoor activities. Easily share your knowledge and experience, except where code 1(c) applies. Be specifically helpful to beginning birders.

4(b) If you witness dishonest birding behavior, evaluate the circumstance, and intervene if you believe it is sensible. When interceding, notify the individual(s) of the improper action, and try, within reason, to have it stopped. If the conduct continues, record it, and inform appropriate people or organizations.

Group Leader Responsibilities [amateur and professional tours and trips]

4(c) Be an excellent ethical role model for the group. Show it through words and example.

4(d) Keep groups to a size that restricts the influence on the environment, and does not interfere with others utilizing the identical location.

4(e) Guarantee everybody in the group knows of and practices this code.

4(f) Learn and notify the group of any special scenarios relevant to the areas being gone to (e.g., no tape recorders enabled).

4(g) Acknowledge that professional trip companies bear a special obligation to put the well-being of birds and the benefits of public knowledge before the company's commercial interests. Preferably, leaders ought to keep track of trip sightings, file uncommon incidents, and send records to suitable organizations.

Please follow this code and distribute and teach it to others. While it might appear repetitive, it bears repeating just for the simple courtesy of other bird watchers in addition to those we are watching!

You have actually got the tools and understand what you should and shouldn't do. Now let's go locate some birds!

Chapter 4: Where to Locate the Birds

The wonderful part about birding is that it can really be done anywhere! You can go to your local park and locate some excellent specimens. If you're traveling, you'll discover a brand-new appreciation of the tunes of birds and what you can discover. You can even see birds in your own backyard! There will be more within this book about backyard birding.

You want to understand what to anticipate in your area. Checklists of birds in your location will tell you this. Lots Of State and National parks near you have checklists of the birds seen in the park. There are numerous sites that have checklists for every single state and province in the United States and Canada in addition to every country on the planet! You can discover other fantastic websites for birding on the internet.

Find out about the habitat each species of bird likes. Do they like to spend their time at the top of a tree or on the soil or on a lake? You ought to understand the songs of the birds in your backyard. Later on, learn the songs of other birds in your part of the nation. To locate a bird, you are going to frequently hear it first.

You might wish to take part in a group of other birders. Birders are extremely friendly and helpful. They are always happy to share their understanding. We were all novices once. Begin by calling the local Audubon Society, the local Nature Center or Parks Commission, or the local Bird Club. In case all else falls short, go to the park with your binoculars. Somebody is sure to strike up a conversation and they may lead you to a whole new group of birding pals.

Try a birding tour or trip. Local bird trips are, in some cases, promoted in the newspapers. These are typically led by park rangers or a local Audubon member. To learn about local trips, you ought to additionally call your local Rare Bird Alert contact number.

After reciting the list of rare birds seen in the location, they typically point out upcoming excursions. The trips might last a morning or the majority of the day. These trips are generally free of charge. You may additionally wish to join a professional guide on tour. Tour guides charge for their services, but they deserve every cent. Birding trips can take you all over the world.

Birds do not regularly hang out in elegant locations; sewage dumps are a favorite. However, you need not begin there. Stroll along the beach, in a meadow, by a brook, or on a path. You'll discover birds en route. One recommendation: stay away from thick woods where birds remain concealed. Open locations with trees or hedges are better. Do not forget the zoo. It most likely has a pond with ducks and other waterfowl, and they are used to having individuals around.

Plan a vacation that consists of birding. Wherever you go, take a look at the birding hot spots ahead of time and include them into your trip. The bimonthly magazine Bird Watcher's Digest notes destinations that accommodate birders, and its posts by amateur birders communicate the thrills of this pastime.

Birds aren't always out on a branch in full view; if it was that simple, this would not be a sport! Species can be discovered at numerous eye levels, from on the ground to in little shrubs, and from on tree trunks to atop skyscrapers. As soon as you know what birds live in your location and when, read about what kind of environment they choose for feeding, reproducing and raising young. Having bird feeders, birdhouses and birdbaths in your backyard definitely makes it simpler to see birds.

There are specific times of day when birds are more active than others, depending upon the species. The very best time to see most birds is normally earlier in the morning; the evening is less effective unless you are trying to find nighttime species, such as owls. Additionally, take notice of the season. Spring and fall migrations are a good time to find birds that fly long distances and stop in your neck of the woods for a rest.

Now that you're equipped with the tools and the basic understanding, how can you recognize the birds you see?

Chapter 5: What Type of Bird is That?

There are numerous various birds out there. You most likely will not have the ability to determine each and every single bird you see. Nevertheless, equipped with some fundamental information, you can most likely narrow down the list and discover that you may have a species worth studying.

What should you search for when identifying birds? Ending up being a professional on visual recognition takes some time and patience. Some groups of birds are a lot easier to definitively recognize than others.

The first thing to keep in mind is: do not make bird recognition hard on yourself. There are 2 basic rules to bear in mind throughout your first couple of months of bird watching: 1) get rid of as many species as possible from consideration before you ever try to recognize anything, and 2) the bird is more than likely a species that frequently appears in your area, not some odd exotic that flew in from a thousand miles away.

Among the simplest ways to exclude birds is to go through your field guide and place an "X" beside those that do not usually occur in your geographical location. Put these aside for the time being. By doing this, you dramatically lower the number of birds you need to stress over identifying, from the 900 birds in your guide to the 300 or so birds that are frequently observed in your area!

By the way, do not stress over marking up your field guide. A field guide personally adapted to meet your requirements is the very best pal you can have when alone in the field. Simply make certain to utilize a pencil or permanent ink so that the words will not smear if you leave the book in the rain or drop it in the mud from time to time.

Another way to get rid of options is to think about the time of year the bird might appear in your area. The range maps featured with field guides show this kind of information. Some novices may even find it beneficial to put colored dots beside birds in their field guides.

For instance, put a red dot beside birds that are year-round residents, put a blue dot beside birds that are just winter visitors, put a green dot beside birds that are summer visitors, and put a black dot beside birds that just travel through due to migration.

CLUES TO IDENTIFICATION

Due to the manner in which some birds skulk about, you 'd assume that they were scared of flaunting their lovely colors and didn't want anybody to recognize them. And this holds true, no doubt, as they need to, in some way, evade predators from both above and below. Frequently, their fast movements allow us just a peek. Still, you will have the ability to recognize even the most secretive bird utilizing the crucial clues to identification explained here. There are 5 standard hints you can look for and listen for that are going to allow you to deal with the bird identification puzzle: 1) the bird's shape, 2) its plumage and pigmentation, 3) its conduct, 4) its habitat choices, and 5) its voice. This might appear like a formidable quantity of information to collect, however, in truth, you typically need only one or two of these hints to recognize a bird.

In some cases, the secret to identification is as simple as understanding which hints to try to find initially when you see an uncommon bird. As your birding capabilities increase, you will have the ability to identify the essential clues with better ease and certainty.

Silhouette - Sizes And Shape

As you end up being acquainted with your field guide, you will have the ability to rapidly classify most birds into families utilizing silhouette alone (keep in mind, each family has a diagnostic size and shape).

This will instantly place you at an advantage compared to the ordinary observer since by putting the bird you see into a specific family, you have actually already narrowed down the possible birds you might be seeing from the 900 in your field guide to just about 15 or so birds - the 15 birds within the family you have actually recognized. As pointed out previously, you can then further get rid of any species in the family that do not appear in your area throughout that season.

You can do this even in the worst of lighting conditions when birds are backlit, in low light, or in shadow. It does not matter. The overall shape is the same. Lots of birds are even recognizable by the outline alone.

Naturally, it will not be simple to perform this task in the beginning. You need to discover how to note all the information about a bird's shape thoroughly. Is the bird big or small, short-legged or long-legged, crested or not crested, plump or slim and sleek, short-tailed or long-tailed? Take note of each and every detail within your field note pad.

The shape of a bird's bill is additionally an exceptionally handy hint that is apparent from a silhouette. Cardinals, finches, and sparrows have short cone-shaped bills. Woodpeckers have chisel-shaped bills for working deadwood. Hawks, eagles, and falcons, meanwhile, have sharp, hooked bills that make quick work of meat. Shorebirds have slim bills of all lengths for penetrating at several depths into the sand.

The beak is a dead giveaway. It shows whether the bird cracks seeds (short, thick beak), drills for grubs (long, pointed beak), picks things off leaves (short, thin beak), etc. Your bird guide can assist you in determining beak shapes. Size is additionally a crucial field mark and field guides do note the size of birds beside photos. Nevertheless, if you do not have some kind of scale in mind, these numbers are of little use. The "ruler" numerous birders utilize in the field is a psychological association of 3 familiar birds with 3 general size classes.

For instance, a house sparrow is 5-6 inches in size, a northern mockingbird is 9-11 inches in size, and an American crow is 17-21 inches in size. Now, utilizing expressions like "larger than a crow" or "tinier than a sparrow," you have an instant impression of the approximate size of any bird. You additionally have an instant context for your field guide in case you associate each of these 3 species with 5, 10, and 20-inch size classes.

Plumage

Plumage qualities are what actually draws a great deal of individuals into bird watching - they like seeing those wonderful colors. The differentiating plumage hints that determine various types are referred to as "field marks." These consist of such things as breast spots, wing bars (thin lines along the wings), eye rings (circles around the eyes), eyebrows (lines over the eyes), eye lines (lines through the eyes) and numerous others.

Some field marks are best seen when a bird remains in flight. A flying northern harrier could be recognized from almost a mile away with great binoculars due to the fact that the bird has an intense white spot on its rump. Some families of birds could be broken into even tinier groups based upon a couple of easy field marks. For instance, warblers are relatively uniformly divided between those that have wing bars and those that do not. So if you see a warbler-like bird, look swiftly to see if it has wing bars. Sparrows, however, can be separated into 2 tinier groups based upon whether or not the breast is streaked. Try to find other broad distinctions for other families.

Behavior

A bird's behavior - how it flies, forages, or typically comports itself - is among the very best hints to its identity.

Hawks have a "considerable" attitude, crows and jays are "gregarious," and cuckoos are ... well, not really. Woodpeckers go up the sides of tree trunks looking for grubs like a lineman scaling a telephone pole.

Flycatchers, on the other hand, would not climb a tree trunk if their lives depended on it. They spend the majority of their time sitting upright on an exposed perch. The moment they see a bug cruising into range, they rapidly dart from their perch, snag the meal, and after that go back to the identical perch or another one close-by.

Finches spend a great deal of their time on the ground looking for fallen seeds, as do mockingbirds, catbirds, and brown thrashers. Some wading birds, like snowy egrets and reddish egrets, are really active foragers and hunt their prey around in shallow waters. Other wading birds, like great blue herons, are less spontaneous and hunt gradually with exceptional patience and stealth.

Even the manner in which a bird props its tail offers some hints regarding which species or family it might be. Wrens typically hold their tails in a cocked position and typically bounce from side to side.

Spotted sandpipers and Louisiana water thrushes bounce their tails and rumps swiftly up and down as if doing a trendy dance step. Several thrushes and flycatchers, meanwhile, move their tails often but gradually, with a wave-like motion.

You can even recognize some birds simply by the way that they fly. The majority of finches and woodpeckers move through the air with an undulating flight pattern, flapping their wings for short bursts and after that tucking them under for a brief rest.

One group of raptors, the buteos or soaring hawks, circle the sky suspended on outstretched wings. The majority of falcons, another group of raptors, fly with solid wing beats and hardly ever hover. Yet another group, the accipiters or bird hawks, generally fly in a straight line with shifting durations of flapping and floating.

Habitat

Even if a range map reveals that a bird appears in your neck of the woods, this does not suggest the bird is going to be common anywhere you go. Birds segregate themselves according to habitat type and are, in some cases, rather fussy in choosing a location as home.

Wading birds and ducks, for instance, choose watery habitats instead of dry upland locations. Pine warblers and brown-headed nuthatches associate mostly with pinewoods and are less common in locations containing a great deal of oaks, hickories, and other deciduous trees. Beginning bird watchers need to typically spend numerous hours in the field before they have the ability to associate various species with various habitat types. You must develop a key to habitats you often visit and keep notes of where you see various species.

Make the habitat key simple in the beginning, utilizing terms such as salt and freshwater marsh, pinelands, deciduous forest, beach, urban area, farm and pastureland, and so on. Then elaborate on this key as you find out how to differentiate amongst various habitat kinds.

You can place abbreviations like "SM" (for saltwater marsh), "PW" (for pinewoods), and "FP" (for farm and pasture) beside the pictures of birds in your field guide after you have some feel for where the birds appear. Many field guides offer this information in the written description; however, this abbreviated system might help you remember the habitats where every bird appears.

Voice

Birds have distinct songs and calls and voice is frequently all that's required to recognize a number of the birds you come across. If each species didn't have a distinct call or song, there would be a great deal of confusion out there when birds attempted to communicate. Just as you can tell that the individual on the other end of the phone is Uncle Bob and not Auntie Edith, so too can you find out how to distinguish the various voices of birds. Listening to recordings assists significantly when you are attempting to understand bird vocalizations. Many are presently available on tape and CD. You can additionally locate them online.

Nevertheless, no matter how many recordings you listen to, there is no alternative to heading out into the field. There's something about the association of voice and bird that aids to fix both in memory. Additionally, bird vocalizations are intricate and no set of recordings can hope to incorporate all the assortment and geographical variations that could be experienced firsthand out in nature.

Keep all of these aspects in your note pad, recording the bird's functions as you observe it. Watch it as long as you can. Jot down your description while it's fresh. Then, search in your field guide for additional identification.

In general, you ought to make an effort to keep the following points in mind when attempting to recognize the birds you see.

Begin by concentrating on those groups that are both common and distinct, and after that, when you see an unfamiliar species, take a visual inventory of its distinct qualities. How big is it? What is the shape of the body? Does it walk, hop, waddle or wade? Notice the shape of its beak. Is it long, narrow, stalky, flat or hooked? Is there a crest on the head? Does the tail extend past the body? Is the tip round, square, forked or fan-shaped? Take a mindful inventory of the colors of the bird. Particularly take a look at the head, wings, and tail. In flight, the color of the back edge of the wing, or speculum, is among the major identifiers for waterfowl.

When the bird moves, take note of its habits. This is frequently as distinct as its physical look. How does it hold its tail? Is it discovered on the ground, set down in trees, or soaring high above? When set down, does it hold its body vertical or horizontal? Does it utilize its tail as a support as in woodpeckers? If it climbs up along the trunk, does it have a tendency to go up the tree or down?

If it lives in and around the water, observe how it swims. Does it simply tip its bill into the water keeping its tail above the surface, or does it dive entirely underwater? When it blasts off, does it leap directly into the air or does it need a long runway to become airborne? If it wades, make a note of how long its legs are. Does it gradually stalk like a heron or swiftly run along the coastline probing with its beak? Does it bob up and down like a dipper or teeter like a spotted sandpiper?

When airborne, does it have a continuous rhythm or does it undulate like a woodpecker? Does it usually fly in a straight line or carry out aerial acrobatics like a swallow? How quickly does it beat its wings? Is it alone or in a flock? Additionally making a note of the habitat and season might aid in recognizing a bird, or at least help to distinguish between 2 comparable species. Birds are typically migratory, appearing in big flocks on open water in the fall and spring. Understanding their habitat and yearly cycles can typically form the last crucial element in recognition.

If it was feeding, figure out if its food was nectar, fruit, bugs, seeds, or other animals.

A couple of other things to think about when recognizing birds:

- It's what you observe initially, yet the color is questionable. A bird's color changes significantly in various light conditions. So do not count on color alone when you try to determine the bird in a guide.

- Check the range. You might believe you have actually recognized the bird, yet make certain it ought to be there. Beginning birders make fantastic finds-- often the only example of a species to be seen in that area. Your birding guide ought to give ranges for various species. Make certain your bird belongs.

- Do not attempt to find a bird just by sound. They're ventriloquists. And do not scan the trees with your binoculars. Rather, look for motion, and after that, aim your binoculars. Quick. Even if you have actually got one of those pesky, flitting warbler species, keep attempting. You'll get it.

- If you simply can't find it, forget it. Remember this guideline: Any bird you didn't see was a robin.

Do not forget to pay special attention to the song of the bird. This might be a primary part of recognizing the bird you have actually seen.

Chapter 6: Bird Watching With Your Ears

A bird does not sing due to the fact that it has an answer. It sings since it has a song.

~ Chinese Proverb

A bird's song can be wonderful music or a shrieking inconvenience. Its tune can help you recognize what sort of bird it is and where to search for it in your field guide. All you need is to tune in to their songs. Each species makes sounds that are distinct, and you can recognize the birds by those sounds just as quickly as you can by their shape or color.

Certainly, there are advantages to birding by ear. You can do it in the dark (a helpful ability for recognizing owls when you're camping). The barred owl, for instance, sounds totally different from any other sound you hear during the night.

A bird concealed in thick summertime foliage will frequently sing out its identity for all who have ears to hear. And although you can see with your eyes just in the direction you happen to be facing, you can hear in all directions at the same time, so you can recognize a bird by its song even when it's behind your back.

We, humans, reside in a separate sensory world from many animals of the earth. Your pet dog, for instance, experiences the world primarily through his nose, while our sense of smell is petty by comparison. It's tough even to think of the sensory impressions taken in by bats or beetles, frogs or fish.

On the other hand, birds' greatest senses are sight and hearing, and they have actually developed ways to interact and to acknowledge their own species by utilizing signals based upon those 2 senses. Due to the fact that we are additionally creatures of sight and sound, we can tap right into all the remarkable distinctions of color and shape that birds embody, and just as naturally, we can value the noises that are so essential in their lives. As you start to acknowledge bird songs, you are going to bring yourself into a whole new dimension of bird watching. You are going to most likely find yourself enthralled by the sing-song voice of the bird outside your window and recognize birds you didn't know you had around you!

Get a field guide to bird songs. Just as you require a book with images to discover what birds look like, you require recordings to discover what they sing like. Thankfully, there are numerous exceptional tapes and CDs of bird songs out there now. You can additionally discover some exceptional resources online for bird songs. Acquaint yourself with these songs and open yourself to an entirely new world of bird watching!

When you hear a bird's song, explain it to yourself in words. You may discover that the white-breasted nuthatch has a nasal sound to his "Yenk, yenk, yenk" song, and that each note of the northern cardinal's song is a slippery, downward slurp, or that the blue jay's call is often loud and extreme, as if the birds were shouting "Burglar!" Making a mental note of such attributes helps you identify the bird when you hear it once more.

Associate a phrase of English with the song, like "Peter, Peter, Peter" for the tufted titmouse. The words are going to remind you of the rhythm, speed, or pitch of the song.

It's ideal when you are able to fit your own words to a bird's song, but feel free to utilize unforgettable expressions others create. The ovenbird is generally reputed to sing out "teacher, Teacher, TEACHER," and it's tough to improve on "Quick, three beers!" for the Olive-sided flycatcher's call. As soon as you ascribe words to a bird's song, the melody sticks with you permanently. Chicago might no longer refer to simply a city in Illinois; it might be the song of that distinct bird you discovered recently.

After you have actually ended up being knowledgeable about a couple of tunes, make a point of listening early in the morning. Throughout the hour before dawn, lots of birds sing. The chorus is beautiful to listen to as a whole, however, it is additionally a pleasure to single out and identify the individual voices in the choir

At any season, you are able to see more birds with your ears than you are able to with your eyes. So why not try tomorrow morning? Sleep with a window open, so that you'll hear the birds singing when you first get up. If you do not understand what they are, try to separate out one tune from the rest. Although the singer might stay a secret to you for a while, it will act as your motivation to find out how to see with your ears. You do not always need to travel to discover birds. You can draw in lots of species of birds to your house-- right in your own yard. What could be better than resting on your porch and pursuing bird watching in the convenience of your own house?

Chapter 7: Backyard Birding

Amongst the fondest and most unforgettable moments of youth are the discoveries of songbirds nesting in the backyard. The distinct, mud-lined nests of robins and their stunning blue eggs mesmerize individuals of all ages. Also, the nesting activities of house wrens, cardinals, chickadees, and other typical birds can promote a long-lasting interest in nature. As you discover how to take pleasure in the charm of birdlife around your house, you might want to enhance the "habitat" in your backyard so that more birds are going to visit your property. You can draw in birds by putting bird feeders, nest boxes, and birdbaths in your backyard, and by planting a variety of trees, shrubs, and flowers. These can offer excellent nesting sites, winter shelter, places to conceal from predators, and natural food supplies that are accessible year-round.

There are a couple of different methods to draw in a variety of birds to your backyard. These can consist of planting particular flowers, setting up a bird feeder, or putting out a birdbath.

You can do backyard birding and bring in birds to your backyard by offering appropriate food, water, and habitats for wild birds, and restricting the use of pesticides. Bushes and thick hedges secure birds from predators, offer perches, and are home to bugs, which are terrific bird food. Vibrant flowers additionally draw in hummingbirds.

It doesn't matter where you live - in an apartment, townhouse or single-family dwelling, in the city, suburban areas or country. Simply stand still and you'll hear them: wild birds. It is tough to envision life without them.

Chapter 8: Bird Feeders

There are a number of elements to think about after you have actually chosen to feed birds in your backyard.

Where do you wish to view your birds? From a kitchen area window, a sliding glass door opening onto a deck, a second-story window?

Choose an area that is simple to get to. When the weather condition is bad and birds are most vulnerable, you might hesitate to fill a feeder that is not in a convenient area near a door or an accessible window. Additionally, select a site where discarded seed shells and bird droppings will not be a cleanup issue.

Put your feeder where the squirrels can't reach. Squirrels end up being an issue when they take control of a bird feeder, frightening the birds and tossing seed all over. Squirrels have actually been known to chew right through plastic and wood feeders.

If you have actually seen squirrels in your area, it is safe to presume they are going to visit your feeder. Think long and hard before you hang anything from a tree limb. Squirrels are extremely nimble, and any feeder hanging from a tree is likely to end up being a squirrel feeder. Over time, a squirrel-proof feeder or any feeder on a pole with a baffle is the least annoying solution. The most reliable squirrel-proof feeder is the pole-mounted metal "house" type.

What type of bird food should you utilize? The hands-down favorite bird seed is a sunflower. It draws in cardinals, woodpeckers, blue jays, goldfinches, purple finches, chickadees, titmice, and nuthatches. Get the black sunflower seeds, often called oil seeds. Birds prefer them to the grey-and-white-striped sunflower seeds sold off the candy rack for individuals, due to the fact that they're higher in oil material. They are softer shelled, thus much easier to crack open. They're additionally more affordable than the grey-and-white ones.

Another important bird seed is niger. Goldfinches love niger. Niger is a black seed, so small and light, you can blow away a handful with a mild breath. Niger is additionally pricey, over a dollar a pound, so you will not wish to lose it. Purchase a hanging tube with small holes, created specifically for niger, and hang it where you can see it from your best viewing window. Up close to the house, even under the eaves, is great. Goldfinches will end up being really tame and will not mind you standing 2 feet far from them, on the other side of the window, while they eat.

Another favorite kind of seed for birds is the safflower, a white seed, a little tinier than a black sunflower seed. Squirrels do not like it. Neither do grackles, blue jays, or starlings. Safflower seeds are exceptionally bitter. Cardinals, titmice, chickadees, and downy woodpeckers chew it like candy, however, so keep an excellent supply available on the platform feeder. The squirrels will not make an effort to go up there too.

White millet is another seed that draws in birds. It is even less expensive than sunflower seeds. Spread it on the ground for sparrows, juncos, and mourning doves.

You can purchase these seeds at feed shops, nurseries, grocery stores, and some hardware stores. It's a great idea to purchase everything except the expensive niger in 50-pound bags and keep them in the garage in mouse-proof metal trash bins.

Don't bother with bags of mixed birdseed. These mixes generally include a great deal of filler, such as red millet. A lot of birds will not consume it. They search through the seeds in the feeder and kick the red millet onto the ground, where, at best, it lies up until it decomposes and becomes quite good fertilizer for the grass. Mixed birdseed is not a bargain. Purchase the seeds you understand your birds want.

When starting up a feeding program, be patient. It might take as long as numerous weeks before the birds find your feeders. While you wait, make certain to keep the feeders filled. Ultimately, the birds are going to come.

Often conscientious individuals are worried about whether feeding the birds i going to hurt the birds. Will the birds end up being dependent on the handouts? And it's frequently encouraged that one needs to just begin feeding birds if certain that the feeding can continue undisturbed.

Nevertheless, the proof shows that feeding is not likely to be detrimental to birds. They do not settle in and dine at simply one location. Goldfinches, for instance, follow a circuit every day, going to a number of feeders and wild food spots, as we understand from studies of banded birds that could be recognized separately.

With numerous families feeding birds, it's not likely that a bird will starve since one feeder goes empty. All the same, birds that enter into your backyard at dusk are starving, and it is bad manners to dishearten visitors! Ensure they have enough to dine on at your pleasure!

Birds like to feed upon hanging suet molds. You can purchase these in various locations, yet this can be particularly enjoyable if you can make them yourself. They're so simple, even the kids can help! Make a simple bird feeder by connecting a brief length of string to a pine cone, covering the pine cone with a suet, lard, or veggie shortening mix (see below), and rolling it in seeds, and after that, suspending it from a tree branch.

Fatty mixture: Mix 1/2 cup suet, lard, or veggie shortening with 2 1/2 cups cornmeal or raw oats up until well mixed. Optional: include dried fruit (sliced up), sliced nuts, and/or 1/4 cup finely sliced leftover meat (just in cold weather).

Hummingbirds drink nectar, which is additionally simple to make yourself. Take 1/4 cup sugar and liquify in boiling water. Place into your hummingbird feeder and see them come! Make sure to alter the nectar frequently as-- specifically in warm weather-- the mix can become rancid and hazardous for the birds. Additionally, hummingbirds tend to delight in red nectar the best, so include a couple of drops of food coloring to the mix!

Do not forget water! The very best way to offer water to your feathered buddies is with a birdbath.

Chapter 9: Backyard Bird Baths

Kindness is a birdbath. Your little circle of tidy, cool water under a leafy branch is a kindness to the birds, since fresh, clean water can, in some cases, be the toughest requirement for birds to come by. And it's a kindness to yourself and your household, too, due to the fact that seeing the birds at the birdbath will bring you exceptional joy.

In fact, a birdbath is among the simplest ways to bring birds up close, where you can get a truly great look at them. You can draw in a lot more species of birds with water than with a feeder.

Bird feeders generally accommodate seed-eaters, such as cardinals, blue jays, and sparrows. Birds that eat bugs or fruit, such as wrens, catbirds, and waxwings, normally do not find anything at the feeder to intrigue them. Yet the birdbath attracts all types of birds, from robins to screech owls. It is going to broaden your awareness of the variety of life.

Commercial birdbaths are available at numerous discount stores and gardening or house improvement shops, however, you can make a birdbath out of practically anything. Simply make certain it supplies what the birds require most-- cool, clear water!

What type of birdbath is ideal? It needs to be shallow - no deeper than 3 inches at the center. It ought to be even shallower at the edge, so that a bird can ease its way in. Lots of commercial bird baths are too deep. If you currently own a deep birdbath, you can place rocks in it to elevate the bottom, though this is going to make it a little tougher to keep clean.

Think about adding a water fountain or something to offer a little bit of a drip. The plinking noise of falling water is a pure invitation to birds. It drastically increases the number of species that go to a birdbath. For instance, hummingbirds would never ever wade into the bath like other birds, due to the fact that they bathe just in flight. However, many have actually watched hummers zipping backward and forward through the drips of a birdbath, timing their flights to ensure that they catch a water drop on their backs on each pass.

There are lots of ways to arrange for a drip. You can run a hose so that it trickles into the water; or set up a little spray water fountain created for birdbaths; or suspend above the bath a bucket that has a 1/2-inch hole in the bottom with a little bit of cloth packed through the hole as a wick.

Additionally, make certain your birdbath is rough bottomed. Birds do not wish to lose their footing, and they are going to be reluctant to utilize a bath with a glazed, slippery bottom. Cement is great. If you currently possess a slick birdbath, you can use the non- skid stickers that are sold for people-baths.

Put your birdbath within view from a window. Do not forget to put yourself in this picture. Put the birdbath where you are able to see it from inside, from your desk, dining room, or kitchen area sink. Place the basin on a pedestal. It's simple to see from your home, simple to clean, and much safer from predators. Additionally, you can purchase a birdbath created to hang from a tree.

Make your birdbath simple to clean and fill up by putting it close enough to reach with a hose. Nevertheless, find your birdbath far from your feeding station, due to the fact that seeds and droppings would soil the water rapidly. Change the water every few days, or perhaps every day in hot weather. Dump it out or squirt it out with the hose. It's an excellent idea to keep a scrub brush outside with gardening tools, so that you can brush out any algae that may start to form.

Put the birdbath where predators can not get to your visitors. Cats, for instance, like to wait below shrubbery or behind a concealing item, and after that, pounce on the birds when they're wet and can't fly well. So put your birdbath at least 5 to 10 feet from such hiding places. Offer the birds an opportunity to see the cat coming. Likewise, supply the birds with an escape path. The perfect place is under some branches that hang down within 2 or 3 feet of the bath. A damp bird can flutter a couple of feet up to the safety of the leaves.

In the event that you follow these directions, soon, a robin is going to land on the rim of your birdbath. He'll dip his bill into the water, and after that, raise his head to let the water run down inside his throat. Then he'll hop in and splash exuberantly. He'll dunk his head and let the water rush over his back. He'll sit and soak.

When he's finished bathing, he'll fly onto the closest branch, where he'll shake off and start to preen his feathers, drawing them one at a time through his bill.

A bird in the bath is the soul of enjoyment. The sight of it, even a chance peek through the window, is going to supply you too with a splash of joy.

Chapter 10: Bird Houses

You may decide you do not want your birds to simply stop by to eat and take a bath. Maybe you 'd like it if they 'd stick around for a while. Try setting up a birdhouse or two.

In the birdhouse industry, there's no such thing as "one size fits all." Choose which bird you wish to draw in, and after that, get a house for that specific bird. Check out any book or catalog and you'll see birdhouses of all shapes and sizes, with perches and without, made from materials you may not have actually considered: recycled paper, gourds, plastic, rubber, pottery, metal and concrete. The appropriate mix of quality materials and style makes a great birdhouse.

Wood is practically the best building component for any birdhouse. It's durable, has great insulating qualities and breathes. Three-quarter-inch thick bald cypress and red cedar are advised. Pine and exterior grade plywood will do, yet they are not as resilient. It makes no difference whether the wood is slab, rough-cut or finished, as long as the interior has actually not been treated with spots or preservatives. Fumes from the chemicals might hurt the birds.

You can embellish the exterior of your birdhouse however you desire. Do you wish for your martins to hang out in a Victorian home or have your cardinals roost in a clubhouse? Anything goes as far as the exterior of your home is concerned. Do not put an aluminum roof on your birdhouse, nevertheless. The glare from the sun will cause birds to shy away. Make sure to supply ventilation, drainage, and simple access for upkeep and checking.

How intricate you make your birdhouse depends upon your own tastes. In addition to where you put the box, essential factors to consider are box height, depth, floor dimensions, diameter of entryway hole and height of the hole above the box flooring.

You ought to provide air vents in bird boxes. There are 2 ways to supply ventilation: leave gaps between the roof and sides of the box, or drill 1/4 inch holes just beneath the roof.

Water ends up being an issue when it sits at the bottom of a birdhouse. A roof with ample slope and overhang provides some safety. Drilling the entryway hole on an upward slant might additionally help keep the water out. Despite the design, driving rain is going to get in through the entryway hole. You can ensure appropriate drainage by removing the corners of the box floor and drilling 1/4 inch holes. Nest boxes are going to last longer if the floors are recessed about 1/4 inch.

Search for the entrance hole on the front panel near the top. A rough surface area both inside and out renders it simpler for the grownups to enter into the box and, when it's time, for the nestlings to climb out.

If your box is made from finished wood, include a number of grooves outside beneath the hole. Open the front panel and add grooves, cleats or wire mesh to the interior. Never ever set up a birdhouse with a perch beneath the entryway hole.

Perches offer starlings, home sparrows and other predators a handy location to wait for lunch. Do not be lured by duplexes or houses that have more than one entryway hole. Besides purple martins, cavity-nesting birds choose not to share a house. While these condos look terrific in your backyard, starlings and house sparrows are inclined to utilize them.

Where you put your birdhouse is as crucial as its design and building. Cavity-nesting birds are really particular about where they live. If you do not have the appropriate habitat, the birds are not most likely to discover your house. You can customize your land to draw in the birds you wish to see by putting out a birdbath, planting fruit-bearing shrubs, incorporating more trees or setting up a pond with a waterfall.

Do not put birdhouses near bird feeders. Houses installed on metal poles are less susceptible to predators than homes nailed to tree trunks or hung from tree limbs.

Utilize no more than 4 little nest boxes or one big box per acre for any one species. Do not place more than one box in a tree unless the tree is very big or the boxes are for various species. If you have really hot summers, deal with the entrance holes of your boxes north or east to make sure you don't overheat the box.

You can additionally draw in some distinct species of birds by merely landscaping your backyard to draw in birds.

Chapter 11: Landscaping Birds

As individuals discover how to take pleasure in the beauty of birds around their house, they might want to improve the "habitat" in their backyard so that more birds are going to visit their property. We have actually currently addressed enhancing their habitat with birdhouses, feeders, and baths. Now let's take a look at planting a range of trees, shrubs, and flowers to draw in birds. These can offer great nesting sites, winter season shelter, places to conceal from predators and natural food goods that are accessible year-round.

Wonderful landscaping isn't just for drawing in in birds. It can increase your property worth, offer natural beauty, and end up being a playground for kids as numerous wildlife is drawn to your backyard.

Landscaping for birds involves 9 fundamental principles:

Food

Every bird species has its own special food requirements that might change as the seasons change. Find out the food habits of the birds you want to draw in. Then plant the suitable trees, shrubs, and flowers to supply the fruits, berries, seeds, acorns, and nectar.

Wate

You might have the ability to double the number of bird types in your backyard by supplying a source of water. A frog pond, water garden, or birdbath is going to get a great deal of bird usage, specifically if the water is dripping, splashing or moving.

Shelter

Birds require places where they can conceal from predators and get away from serious weather conditions. Trees (including dead ones), shrubs, tall grass and birdhouses supply exceptional shelter.

Diversity

The very best landscaping plan is one that consists of a range of native plants. This helps draw in the most bird species.

4 Seasons

Provide the birds with food and shelter throughout the year by planting a range of trees, shrubs and flowers that supply year-round rewards.

Arrangement

Effectively set up the various habitat parts in your backyard. Think about the impacts of prevailing winds (and snow drifting), so your backyard will be protected from extreme winter weather.

Protection

Birds must be protected from unneeded death. When picking the positioning of bird feeders and nest boxes, consider their ease of access to predators. Picture windows can additionally be dangerous for birds. They tend to fly straight at windows when they see the reflection of trees and shrubs.

A network of parallel, vertical strings spaced 4 inches apart could be put on the outside of windows to prevent this issue. Be cautious about the sorts of herbicides and pesticides utilized in your backyard. Use them just when needed and strictly according to label directions. As a matter of fact, try gardening and lawn care without utilizing pesticides. Details may be found in gardening books at the library.

Hardiness Zones

When thinking about plants foreign to your area, consult a plant hardiness zone map, discovered in many garden brochures. Make certain that the plants you desire are ranked for the winter hardiness zone classification of your area.

Soils and Topography

Consult your neighborhood garden center, university or county extension office to have your soil checked. Plant species are frequently adjusted to specific kinds of soils. If you understand what kind of soil you have, you can recognize the kinds of plants that are going to grow best in your yard.

7 kinds of plants are essential as bird habitat:

Conifers

Conifers are evergreen trees and shrubs that consist of pines, spruces, firs, arborvitae, junipers, cedars, and yews. These plants are essential as escape cover, winter shelter and summertime nesting sites. Some additionally supply sap, fruits and seeds.

Grasses and Legumes

Grasses and legumes can offer cover for ground-nesting birds, but just if the area is not cut throughout the nesting season. Some grasses and legumes offer seeds too. Native prairie grasses are ending up being progressively popular for landscaping purposes.

Nectar-- producing Plants

Nectar-producing plants are popular for bringing in hummingbirds and orioles. Flowers with tubular red corollas are specifically appealing to hummingbirds. Other trees, shrubs, vines and flowers additionally can offer nectar for hummingbirds.

Summer-fruiting Plants

This classification consists of plants that generate fruits or berries from May through August. In the summertime, these plants can bring in brown thrashers, catbirds, robins, thrushes, waxwings, woodpeckers, orioles, cardinals, towhees and grosbeaks. Instances of summer-fruiting plants are different species of cherry, chokecherry, honeysuckle, raspberry, serviceberry, blackberry, blueberry, grape, mulberry, plum and elderberry

Fall-fruiting Plants

This landscape part consists of shrubs and vines whose fruits ripen in the fall. These foods are essential both for migratory birds that accumulate fat reserves prior to migration and as a food source for non-migratory species that need to go into the winter in excellent physical condition. Fall-fruiting plants consist of dogwoods, mountain ash, winter-berries, cotton easters, and buffalo-berries.

Winter-fruiting Plants

Winter-fruiting plants are those whose fruits stay connected to the plants long after they initially end up being ripe in the fall. A lot of them are not tasty up until they have actually frozen and thawed lots of times. Examples are shiny black chokecherry, Siberian and "red splendor" crabapple, snowberry, bittersweet, sumacs, American highbush cranberry, eastern and European wahoo, Virginia creeper, and Chinaberry

Nut and Acorn Plants

These consist of oaks, hickories, buckeyes, chestnuts, butternuts, walnuts and hazels. A range of birds, like jays, woodpeckers and titmice, eat the meats of damaged nuts and acorns. These plants additionally contribute to a great nesting habitat.

How do you get going now that you're equipped with this substantial knowledge of plants that draw in birds? Your aim will be to plant a variety of trees, shrubs and flowers that are going to bring in birds. If you plan thoroughly, it can be affordable and enjoyable for the entire family.

Initially, set your priorities. Choose what kinds of birds you want to draw in, and after that, develop your strategy around the requirements of those species. Speak with buddies and neighbors to learn what types of birds often visit your area. Participate in a local bird club meeting and speak to local birdwatchers about how they have actually brought in birds to their backyards.

Whenever possible, utilize plants native to your area. Check with the botany department of a close-by college or university or with your state's natural heritage program for lists of trees, shrubs, and wildflowers native to your location. Utilize this list as a starting point for your landscape strategy.

These plants are naturally adjusted to the environment of your area and are a great, long-lasting investment. Lots of native plants are both wonderful for landscaping functions and outstanding for birds. If you include normative plant species in your strategy, make certain they are not considered "intrusive insects" by plant specialists. Have a look at the bird books in your public library.

Sketch an illustration of your home as a map to start with. Sketch on your map the plants you want to include. Draw trees to a scale that represents three-fourths of their mature width, and shrubs at their complete, mature width. This is going to help you work out how many trees and shrubs you require.

There is a propensity to include many trees, which means that, ultimately, your backyard will be mainly shaded. Make certain to leave open sunny sites where flowers and shrubs can grow. Choose just how much cash you can spend and the time span of your project. Do not try to do too much at the same time. You may try a five-year development plan.

Review the 7 plant parts explained formerly. Which parts are currently present? Which ones are missing? Keep in mind that you are attempting to supply food and cover through all 4 seasons. Establish a list of plants that you believe will supply the missing habitat parts.

Lastly, go to it! Begin your plantings and include your whole family so they can all feel they are helping wildlife. Attempt taking photos of your backyard from the very same spots every year to record the cultivation of your plants.

Keep your landscaping looking terrific! Keep your brand-new trees, shrubs and flowers sufficiently watered and keep your planting areas weed-free by use of landscaping film and wood chips or shredded bark mulch. This avoids making use of herbicides for weed control. If issues arise with your plants, seek advice from a local nursery, garden center or county extension agent.

CONCLUSION

Birding is not the simplest sport on the planet to master, however, it is certainly among the most fulfilling. To offset those very first outings when you flipped through your field guide with aggravation, there will be several years' worth of enjoyable and appealing field trips. You see birders experiencing something brand-new each time they go out. Even if they do not see a brand-new species for the very first time, they may see a brand-new behavior, hear a brand-new vocalization, or simply explore a new and wild corner of Florida. They may even encounter something surprising, like an uncommon European bird that in some way strayed far from home.

The continuous variety and difficulty of birding are 2 crucial attractions, but so too is the friendship. About 42 million individuals in the United States are casual bird watchers, feeding and observing birds around their homes. A much tinier number, around 17 million, take tours for the main purpose of watching birds. Still, that's a great deal of individuals poking their heads into bushes and craning their necks towards the sky. Birding is always filled with new individuals and new adventures.

Beginning birding will have its times of irritation, however, if you give it a good shot and discover the fundamentals, you are going to be hooked!

Birding is a mission. You set out to see birds - yet the reward you return with can just be referred to as joy. Discovering how to bird resembles getting a lifetime ticket to the theater of nature.

The essential thing to keep in mind if you are a novice is, the more time you spend taking a look at the birds, the more you will comprehend them and come to enjoy them. Do not be put off by the typical jibes from buddies or associates (yes, there will still be some individuals who can not comprehend why you are captivated by birds), just do what you were going to do and impress yourself and everybody around you!

I hope that you enjoyed reading through this book and that you have found it useful. If you want to share your thoughts on this book, you can do so by leaving a review on the Amazon page. Have a great rest of the day.

Made in the USA
Middletown, DE
17 July 2020